Party

A comedy

Tom Basden

Samuel French — London
www.samuelfrench-london.co.uk

© 2010 by Tom Basden

Rights of Performance by Amateurs are controlled by Samuel French Ltd, 52 Fitzroy Street, London W1T 5JR, and they, or their authorized agents, issue licences to amateurs on payment of a fee. **It is an infringement of the Copyright to give any performance or public reading of the play before the fee has been paid and the licence issued.**

The Royalty Fee indicated below is subject to contract and subject to variation at the sole discretion of Samuel French Ltd.

> Basic fee for each and every
> performance by amateurs   Code F
> in the British Isles

The Professional Rights in this play are controlled by CASAROTTO RAMSAY & ASSOCIATES LTD, Waverley House, 7-12 Noel Street, London W1F 8GQ.

The publication of this play does not imply that it is necessarily available for performance by amateurs or professionals, either in the British Isles or Overseas. Amateurs and professionals considering a production are strongly advised in their own interests to apply to the appropriate agents for written consent before starting rehearsals or booking a theatre or hall.

The right of Tom Basden to be identified as author of this work has been asserted by him in accordance with Section 77 of the Copyright, Designs and Patents Act 1988

ISBN 978 0 573 12202 6

Please see page iv for further copyright information

PARTY

First presented at The Assembly Rooms, George Street, Edinburgh on 6th August 2009 with the following cast:

Jones	Tom Basden
Phoebe	Katy Wix
Duncan	Tim Key
Jared	Jonny Sweet
Mel	Anna Crilly
Short Coat	Nick Mohammed

Directed by Philip Breen
Designed by Max Jones

It was subsequently presented at the Arts Theatre, London, in March 2010 with the same cast.

COPYRIGHT INFORMATION

(See also page ii)

This play is fully protected under the Copyright Laws of the British Commonwealth of Nations, the United States of America and all countries of the Berne and Universal Copyright Conventions.

All rights including Stage, Motion Picture, Radio, Television, Public Reading, and Translation into Foreign Languages, are strictly reserved.

No part of this publication may lawfully be reproduced in ANY form or by any means — photocopying, typescript, recording (including video-recording), manuscript, electronic, mechanical, or otherwise—or be transmitted or stored in a retrieval system, without prior permission.

Licences for amateur performances are issued subject to the understanding that it shall be made clear in all advertising matter that the audience will witness an amateur performance; that the names of the authors of the plays shall be included on all programmes; and that the integrity of the authors' work will be preserved.

The Royalty Fee is subject to contract and subject to variation at the sole discretion of Samuel French Ltd.

In Theatres or Halls seating Four Hundred or more the fee will be subject to negotiation.

In Territories Overseas the fee quoted above may not apply. A fee will be quoted on application to our local authorized agent, or if there is no such agent, on application to Samuel French Ltd, London.

VIDEO-RECORDING OF AMATEUR PRODUCTIONS

Please note that the copyright laws governing video-recording are extremely complex and that it should not be assumed that any play may be video-recorded for whatever purpose without first obtaining the permission of the appropriate agents. The fact that a play is published by Samuel French Ltd does not indicate that video rights are available or that Samuel French Ltd controls such rights.

CHARACTERS

Jones
Phoebe
Duncan
Jared
Mel
Short Coat

The action takes place in a garden shed

Time — the present

PARTY

Inside a shed

There are two small windows in the back wall and a doorway R. *A lightbulb hangs from the ceiling. Jones, Phoebe and Duncan sit around a rickety table* L. *Jared stands by a plush, comfortable armchair, the others sit on fold-out or plastic garden chairs, except Mel who sits on a wheelie office chair to Jared's immediate left, by the door, next to a filing cabinet. There is a pot of coffee on the cabinet. Next to Jared is a flipchart. On it reads "credit crunch??". The table in front of Phoebe is covered in papers and pens. On top of that is her BlackBerry, a Thomas the Tank Engine money box, a large glass jug of water and a screw-top bottle of red wine. They each have an empty glass in front of them of different sizes. Everyone is dressed relatively casually, except Duncan, who wears a suit and a tie that has pictures of skeletons having sex on it. By Jared's chair is a small box*

As the Lights come up, Jared, Mel, Phoebe and Jones all have a hand in the air. Duncan looks at this. They stare at Duncan expectantly. He notices and finally raises his hand

Jared OK. Good. Five.

They drop their arms

All those against?
Jones (*beat*) We've all voted for.
Jared Yes, but I've got to go through it all anyway, otherwise the vote's not valid.

No arms raised. Beat

None against. Any abstaintions?
Mel How can there be any abstentions?
Jared Abstaintions.
Mel It's abstentions.
Jared The word is to abstain.
Mel But it's pronounced abstentions.

Phoebe There are no abstentions, Jared.
Jared Right, no abstaintions. So the vote is carried that we're all in favour of China.

A sense of release. Phoebe shuffles some papers. Duncan doesn't really know what's just happened. Jones stands

Jones What's the next country on the spreadsheet?
Phoebe Um ... climate change.
Jones What? How did that get there?
Phoebe Well it's alphabetical.
Mel Well it shouldn't be alphabetical. We should be sticking with foreign policy.
Phoebe My dad bought a cheap version of Excel and it automatically —
Jared Just find another country please, Phoebe.
Phoebe Muslims?
Mel That's not a country either.

Jones sits back down

Jones It'll do. It's foreign policy.
Mel Not really.
Phoebe They are mostly foreign.
Mel Well not to each other.
Jared OK — let's just do this then please? Let's just quickly get a reading on this one.
Phoebe I'm for them.
Mel Yes, I think we're all for them.
Jared Oh great, that was easy. Shall we vote on —
Jones Well hang on, it kind of depends on which ones.
Phoebe Exactly. I was going to say that.
Jared Ah right, so we're not for them all?
Jones No way.
Phoebe Yes, I'm not for them all just because, you know, some of them support 9/11 and 7/7. And there was the shoe-bomber.
Mel I'm very much against terror.
Phoebe Yes, as am I.
Mel But I'm also very much against the war on terror.
Phoebe Oh yes.
Jared Did you say shoe-bomber, Phoebes? Just now. What's a shoe-bomber?
Phoebe He hid a bomb in his shoe.
Jared No!

Phoebe He did.
Jones That's from a film isn't it?
Jared Come on, Phoebes. Even if he was wearing wellies, it would be very hard to fit a bomb in a shoe.
Jones I've seen that film. It's got Richard Gere in it.
Jared Big fan of Richard Gere.
Mel He's got lovely kind eyes, hasn't he?
Jared Yes, he has.
Phoebe Well if it is a film, then it's based on a true story.
Jones I wouldn't have thought so, Phoebe. There's a scene where Gere manages to clone his own arm.
Phoebe They might have jazzed it up a bit.
Jared This film sounds brilliant.
Jones I didn't see the end.
Phoebe Richard Reid! The shoe-bomber's name was Richard Reid!
Jared Well then he doesn't sound like he was a Muslim anyway, so it's probably not relevant. Let's just quickly get a rough answer to this.
Mel Well we need to find out what's from a film and what's proper terrorism.
Jared Yes, I think that goes without saying, Mel.
Jones I mean, there's not enough being done!
Jared OK. Yes. Good.
Mel What? Where?
Jones In, you know, areas of high concentration, of, you know Muslim ... strongholds.
Mel Strongholds?
Jared Well not strongholds.
Jones No not strongholds. I don't mean strongholds, I mean, you know Bradford.
Jared Yes. Bradford. Write down Bradford, Phoebe.
Phoebe Bradford isn't foreign policy.
Mel Have you ever been to Bradford, Martin?
Jones There are a lot of Muslims there, Mel.
Mel Yes, I know, but how do you know the situation if you've not been?
Jones I don't need to go somewhere to know if there are a lot of Muslims somewhere!
Mel Snappy.
Jones Well, I will be snappy if I'm not allowed to have any bloody coffee.

Mel shields the coffee on the cabinet

Phoebe You're not allowed to have coffee.

Jones I know!
Jared Calm down please. You're right about Bradford anyway, Jonesy. There are a lot of Muslims there.
Jones Thank you.
Phoebe But are they the good type or the bad type?

Beat. This alarms them a bit

Jared Right. I think we're sort of edging towards dodgy territory there. Let's just conclude that.
Phoebe That there are a lot of Muslims in Bradford?
Mel We need to say something else I think.
Phoebe (*after a beat*) Most of them are non-violent.
Jared Well don't put that.
Phoebe Why not?
Jared It feels a bit offensive.
Phoebe I don't see how. If anything it's a compliment.
Jared Yes, OK, fine, but don't use the word "them".
Phoebe Really?
Mel "Them" is very offensive.
Phoebe Right. Those? Shall I put "those"?
Jared No that's —
Mel They.
Phoebe Most of they?
Mel It feels less offensive.
Jared Well it's better than "them".
Duncan Um ... Jared, obviously, don't mean to interrupt, but Jones did mention that there'd be um ... a cake, and obviously, I'm not —
Jared Don't tell me you're only here for the cake, Duncan.

They all laugh and try to resume the conversation

Duncan No, no, this is what I'm saying: this is all great fun and I'm enjoying myself no end, but Jones did say there'd be a lemon drizzle, and I was just checking that you hadn't forgotten or —
Mel Oh for God's sake.
Duncan What?
Mel So what if there's not a cake?
Jared I didn't say there wasn't a cake.
Duncan So there is a cake?
Mel Does it matter if there's a cake or not?
Duncan I was just told there'd be one was the thing.
Jones For what it's worth I could go a slice of cake.

Party

Duncan Well this is it.
Jones It'd be nice.
Duncan It'd be lovely.
Jared We'll stop concentrating if we have cake.
Duncan I actually tend to concentrate better after cake.
Mel Well I don't, thank you very much. Sweet things exhaust me.
Duncan OK. So maybe I could have my slice now and then —
Phoebe We'll get the cake when we've got to halfway.
Duncan Are we not halfway?
Phoebe Clearly not.
Duncan Right. Sorry. Carry on.
Jared Yes. Um ...
Mel What have you got on your tie?
Duncan Oh — it's er ... sort of skeletons having sex.
Jared OK. Let's get back on —
Duncan Also, Jared, while we're stopped, I was going to say before that I don't think I quite understood what I just voted for.
Mel How can you not understand that, Duncan? Are you in favour of China?
Duncan Well, I suppose.
Phoebe Well then.
Duncan But, what — I mean, in what way?
Jared As a concept.
Mel As a country.
Jared As a concept country.
Duncan What's a concept country?
Jared Don't worry about that, Duncan. It's more like, if I was China, would you be my friend?
Mel Well it's not as simple as that, Jared.
Duncan Because you know, there's Tiananmen Square and Tibet and things aren't there?
Jared Well, yes, there are but —
Phoebe And Burma.
Jared Myamar.
Phoebe Sorry?
Jared It's pronounced Myamar.
Phoebe What is?
Jared Burma.
Mel It's not pronounced Myanmar, that's a different name.
Jared Sure. I know that. But, in general, Duncan, we're behind them.
Duncan Just because, sorry, China have got a bit of a human rights record haven't they?
Jared Well yes and no.

Jones Mainly yes.
Jared There are so many people there though.
Mel I hardly think that's a defence.
Jared Well ... you know, I can imagine though, if I was China, and there were a billion of me, then ——
Mel Will you stop comparing yourself to China!
Jared Uh-huh. Yup.
Phoebe What sort of things have they done?
Jones Um ... killing, pillaging ——
Phoebe What's pillaging?
Jones It's — like somewhere between rape and theft.
Jared And it happens in villages.
Duncan Also — they have these sort of mobile um ... death vans. Like mobile libraries, but, without ... books and with, you know, death equipment.
Phoebe (*after a beat*) I'm no longer in favour of China.
Jared Yes, because you're focusing on the negatives, Phoebe.
Phoebe Well what are the positives?
Jared Well ... the cuisine. The technology.
Jones The cuisine?
Jared Yes, the cuisine, Jonesy. It's bloody delicious.
Mel I don't think that ——
Jared Look, China are going to rule the world one day. There I've said it.
Duncan Are they?
Jared Yes, Duncan. They are.
Jones But what does that mean though?
Jared It means, be nice to them, Jonesy.
Jones But, no I mean, the phrase "rule the world" doesn't mean anything anymore does it?
Mel I think you'll find it does.
Jones Yes, but, you know, in fifty years' time we're not going to be reading papers in Chinese and stuff are we?
Phoebe Oh God, I hope not, I've heard it's an incredibly difficult language to learn.
Mel Well it's tonal, Phoebe, so it's all about sounds rather than words.
Phoebe Oh right.
Duncan Like, sort of ... birdsong?
Mel More advanced, Duncan.
Jones Well look, I don't even like the cuisine or the human rights policy.
Phoebe Nor me. It's too glutinous.
Mel Yes, strike the China vote from the minutes please, Phoebe.

Jared Tut. I really want us to be in favour of China.
Mel Well we're not.
Jared Why did you have to open that up again, Duncan? That was completely sewn up.
Duncan Oh sorry.
Jones Well don't blame Duncan.
Duncan Sorry, Jared.
Jared No, well, what's the next country we're voting on, Phoebe?
Phoebe The Netherlands slash Holland.
Duncan Are we ... sorry, are we going to do a vote like this for every country?
Jared Was going to, yes.
Duncan It's just ... how many are there to do?
Jared Fifty-seven.
Duncan And so far today we've done ...
Jared China. Muslims.
Duncan Right, just it's ... already ten to eight.
Jared You're saying we should speed up?
Duncan Um ... no. Don't mind. Is this how it's done then?
Jared What's done?
Duncan Whatever it is you're doing.
Mel Forming our foreign policy.
Duncan Yeah, that.
Mel Well, at the moment, we effectively do whatever America tells us to do. It's frankly appalling.
Jones Oh God, not this again. I am firmly behind Barack Obama.
Mel You wish you were.
Jones What the hell is that supposed to mean?
Mel You fancy him.
Jones Well that's a pathetic thing to say.
Jared Stop this you two. Jonesy does not "fancy" Barack Obama, Mel. As well you know. He just wore that T-shirt a lot last year ... and made that collage. And we're not on America yet so don't ——
Mel We're anti America.
Jones We're pro America ——
Phoebe Oh. America's not on the spreadsheet.
Jared That's a bit of an oversight.
Phoebe Actually, it's fine, I can just change Armenia quite simply.
Jared Oh good idea.
Mel So we don't discuss Armenia?
Phoebe We probably should discuss Armenia.
Mel I insist that we discuss Armenia.
Phoebe So shall I not change Armenia?

Jones Does anyone know anything about Armenia?

Beat

Mel (*quietly*) The Balkans.

Beat

Jones Apart from that it may or may not be part of the Balkans.
Mel Do they have orphans there?
Jones I don't think they're famous for them.
Duncan I like The Netherlands slash Holland. If that helps.
Jared No — let's — let's change focus. Foreign policy isn't working because of a lack of actual um ... knowledge about things like Armenia, which is no-one's fault.
Duncan I've actually been to Holland.
Jared We'll come back to Holland, Duncan — it's not going anywhere.
Duncan Well, funny you should say that, it's actually sinking at a rate of eleven feet per century.

Phoebe gets a text message on her BlackBerry. Jared snatches her phone from the table and stands up

Jared Phones should be off.
Phoebe Give it back.
Jared No, I'm turning it off. Who's "Short Coat"?

Phoebe stands up. She is suddenly very serious

Phoebe Give it to me at once.
Jones What does it say?
Phoebe Do not you dare read that!
Mel Who's Short Coat?
Phoebe He's ... someone I met on Wednesday night.
Mel What's his name?
Phoebe I don't know.
Mel Why do you call him Short ——?
Phoebe He wears a Short Coat!

Jared reads the message

Jared He thinks he might have given you something?

Party   9

Beat. Everyone's aghast

Duncan He put that in a text?
Jared Yeah, like a keycard or something.
Phoebe Right. Yes. Good.
Jared He wants to pick it up.
Phoebe Give it to me. I'll deal with it.

Phoebe takes the phone and starts texting

Jones Why have you got his keycard?
Phoebe Just by mistake, I ... I've got the keycard to his halls. Just ... it was a mistake.
Duncan Ooh. Is that a BlackBerry?
Phoebe Yes.
Duncan Wow. Are there lots of different kinds or ——?
Phoebe I don't know, Duncan, all BlackBerries look the same to me.
Jones Well that's racist.
Phoebe No it isn't.
Jones It nearly is.
Jared Come on, we're not getting anywhere fast here.
Duncan Sorry. I feel like it's my fault.
Jared No, Duncan — it's ——
Mel He's definitely a factor.
Duncan I feel like a factor.
Mel I mean whose friend is he anyway?
Jones Mine, sort of ——
Jared Guys! Please. Duncan — don't you sweat it, mate. You're just, showing your inexperience a little bit in the ... debates.
Duncan Oh. Am I?
Mel Yes, you are.
Duncan Sorry — I'm not really sure what I'm doing wrong ——
Jared OK — so let's just walk you through it slowly. We take an issue like ... Mel?

Mel opens a drawer in the filing cabinet

Mel (*reading*) The death penalty.
Jared An easier one. For Duncs.

She opens the drawer above

Mel Climate change.

Jared Yes, good, so then we discuss that.
Duncan Oh right.

Beat. They wait for Duncan to speak

Jared So ... what do you think about the climate change?
Duncan Right.
Jared Duncan!
Duncan Well I don't know much about it.
Jared Right, OK, perfect, so we'll ... um ... guys, help me out here, tell Duncan what to think about climate change.
Phoebe Well what do you know about it, Duncan?
Duncan Oh right. Well I guess ... weather.

Jared takes a board pen and flicks the flipchart on a page to a blank one

Jared Good. Good stuff. I'll get these down. This is called a brainstorm, Duncan.
Duncan Right-o.

Jared writes "whether"

Jared So we can brainstorm, discuss and then vote you see.
Duncan Yes. Great.
Jared So, whether. What next?
Duncan I meant more, like *the* weather.
Jared Oh right, I thought you meant whether ... or not it was happening.
Mel Of course it's happening, Jared. No one thinks it's not happening.
Jones Some people don't believe in climate change. Like Clarkson and Johnny Ball.
Phoebe So how do they explain winter?
Jones Well because ... climate change doesn't just mean ... the seasons. Does it?
Jared No.
Jones No.

Jared writes "weather"

Jared So, sort of bad weather.
Duncan Well I meant more ... hot weather.
Jared Yes. OK. Any more, Duncs?

Party

Duncan Icecaps.
Jared Good. Icecaps and of course ... bergs.

Jared writes "Icecaps / bergs"

Jones Any more, Duncan?
Duncan I think I'm out.
Mel Brilliant.
Jared That's fine, Duncs. Good eff. So we've got weather, ice-caps and icebergs.
Duncan Ooh, actually, Leonardo DiCaprio.
Jared Why Duncan? Because of *Titanic*?
Duncan No, because he campaigns against climate change.
Jared Oh right. OK, Duncan. Good.

Jared writes "Leonardo D Caprio"

Mel It's D-ICaprio, it's not just D.
Jared It's an initial.
Mel No it isn't.
Jared Well what is it then?
Jones It's not just D, Jared.
Jared I thought it was like John F Kennedy or Jesus H Christ.
Jones Jesus H Christ isn't his actual name though.
Jared Of course it is, Jonesy.
Jones So what does H stand for?
Jared Well, it'll be a biblical name like you know ... Herod.
Phoebe Oh it can't be Herod surely, after all he did.
Jared No, all right, Phoebe, it probably isn't Herod, but it'll be something in that ballpark.
Mel Jesus didn't have a middle name, Jared. He had a Christian name.
Jared Oh — no one's disputing that, Mel. They don't come much more Christian than Jesus.
Duncan So um ... is this all part of the brainstorming then?
Jared Well um ... the point is we're anti climate change. So we can move on to the discussion.

Jared writes "Anty"

Mel Yes exactly.
Duncan Are we anti?
Jared Yes, Duncan, as the brainstorming sort of indicates.
Mel Very anti.

Jones So anti, that you have a car, Mel.
Mel Excuse me, I pay far more tax for having a car than you do. Us motorists are constantly —
Jones Your car hardly counts as a motor. It's more like a disability scooter.
Phoebe Well that's not very nice.
Mel Next time I see you on your shitty bike, I will run you over with it, then we'll see who needs the disability scooter.
Jones That's much worse than what I said!
Jared OK, steady on, Mel, that's a bit —
Jones Firstly, I can cycle faster than your 2 CV, and secondly, your car is so pathetic, it couldn't kill a child.

Phoebe writes

Mel Of course it could.
Jared OK guys, I don't think we should be discussing whether or not Mel's car could or could not kill a child. Don't put that conversation in the minutes, Phoebe — it's a PR nightmare waiting to come true.
Duncan I think it could kill a child.
Mel Thank you, Duncan.
Jared And we've put a lid on that topic, Duncan. We're not going to test it out, so unless Mel has a serious accident involving a child, we shan't find out anyway.
Duncan So, is that the end of the discussion then?
Jared Well, um ... yes, let's vote. All those for stopping climate change!

Mel puts her hand up. Followed by Phoebe and Jones. Duncan then follows suit

Good. Five.

They put their hands down

All those against?

Duncan raises his hand again

Mel There are none against!
Jared All right, Mel, fine, we'll —
Jones Well, Duncan's voted against.
Duncan I can sort of see both sides.

Party 13

Jared I think in that case you're an abstaintion.
Mel Abstention.
Jared And then that can then go in our party manifesto. You see, Duncs?
Duncan Yes, sort of.
Phoebe I think these issues are all a bit complex for Duncan.
Duncan Could be. I've not really been to a party like this before is all.
Mel What do you mean?
Duncan This is more talking than most other parties I've been to. And voting. (*After a beat*) Although we had to vote at my mum's fortieth for whether or not Uncle Paul should be asked to leave.
Phoebe This is a political party, Duncan.
Duncan Oh. Yes. What?
Mel We've formed a political party.
Duncan Yes. Really?
Jared What did you think we were doing, Duncan?
Duncan I don't — I mean, I thought it was more like a sort of normal party. Like a ... gathering.
Mel Is that why you brought wine?
Jones What had your Uncle Paul done?
Duncan Sorry?
Jones To get asked to leave?
Duncan He does this thing where he makes stink balloons.
Jared My God — what are they?
Mel I think we can imagine what they are.
Jared I can't.
Duncan Sorry, Jared — can I just ask — how? I mean — you can just do that then, can you? You can just form a party?
Jared Yes.
Duncan I see. (*After a beat*) You don't need any ... adults to be involved?
Mel We are adults.
Duncan Oh. Yes, I know, legally. But we're not ... adults.
Mel Yes we are.
Duncan Right.
Mel How much did you explain to him?
Jones I said about the party stuff. You know. Just get off his back.
Duncan What's the party called then?
Jones Ugh.
Mel Well that's still to be decided actually Duncan.
Duncan Oh. Why's that?
Phoebe Because we've got lots of different ideas.

Duncan (*getting out a piece of card*) Right, 'cos looking at the invite — it's confusing when you haven't got a name for it. I mean, I suppose you've got a picture of Big Ben on there, but —

Mel Thank you, Duncan. Exactly what I've been saying. It's very hard to brand the party or make people remember its name, if we don't have a name.

Phoebe Yes, I agree with that.

Jones I don't think we should vote on a name again.

Jared Let's go for it. I'm feeling really good about it. Also — I've got a new one I'd like to throw into the mix.

Duncan Oh great.

Mel Yes, come on.

Phoebe Brill.

Jared OK. Good. This'll be more your scene I think, Duncs. You'll be in your depth with this. Here's a list of the five suggested names thus far. (*To Jones*) In no particular order.

Jones relaxes

The Social Justice Party ...

Beat. Jones blows a raspberry

Mel Oi.

Jones It's a crap name.

Jared None of that please. Put a lid on that. The next one is The Righteous Party.

Mel Sounds like The Righteous Brothers.

Jones No it doesn't. That ended with the word Brothers!

Mel It's stupid.

Jones You're stupid.

Mel Really clever.

Jones I know I am.

Jared OK. Guys. Please. Stop ... doing that. The next one is Gladios.

Duncan What's that?

Jared It's Latin for sword.

Jones Is that your new name?

Jared Sure is.

Jones Like Veritas?

Jared No, very different to Veritas in fact.

Jones Same type of name though.

Jared Well ... yes, but then also no, because we stand for completely different things to Veritas.

Party   15

Duncan What's Veritas?
Jones It's Latin.
Duncan What for?
Jared It's Latin for very. The fourth one is The Liberal Humanist Party ...

Beat. They inhale

> Which was put forward by Elaine last week, and to be honest, we may as well strike it from this list, because she will not be coming back here.

Awkward pause. Jared stares at them defiantly

Duncan What happened to Elaine?

Further pause

Jones Jared grabbed ——
Jared It was dark.
Jones All right.
Mel It wasn't that dark.
Jared It was dark and I thought it was the door handle.
Mel It was a bit high for the door handle ——
Jared Look, forget Elaine. We've got you now, Duncan. You're our fifth man.
Duncan Oh. Is that why you drafted me in, because you were down to four members?
Jared To stop two against twos in the voting — yes exactly.
Jones And ... obviously with your new dad ——
Jared (*cutting him off*) The next one is ——
Duncan What? My new dad?
Jared It doesn't matter.
Duncan No, what, tell me.
Jones It's fine, Jared, we need to mention this anyway. Duncan, your title at the moment is Communication Tsar.
Phoebe What?
Mel I didn't vote for that.
Jared Seriously, it's a good idea.
Duncan Wow really?
Jared Absolutely.
Duncan Communications are ... what?
Jones No, Duncs, Communication Tsar.
Duncan Are they?

Jones Yes, but — as in the Russian royal family.
Duncan Oh my God, what?
Jared Like the Russian Tsar.
Duncan Are they?
Mel For God's sake.
Duncan Sorry, I feel like I'm not getting something.
Mel If you can't communicate what his role means to him, it suggests he probably shouldn't be the Communication Tsar.
Duncan Sorry, everyone.
Mel And why the hell have you made him that?
Jones Seriously, shut up.
Phoebe Yes I agree, it's a serious position —
Mel We don't even want him here.
Jared Girls, please —
Mel Girls?
Phoebe Did you just say girls?
Jared Well, you know.
Mel Oh I'm sorry, I didn't know this was 1950.
Phoebe You shouldn't objectify us because we're women.
Jones He wasn't doing that!
Jared I don't even know how to do that!

A full scale argument develops. The four of them shout for about a minute. It is almost entirely incomprehensible, except where Jared calls the party "Gladios" and the others tell him it's not called that

Jones (*finally, yelling above the din*) Duncan's new dad owns a printing shop, so we thought we'd put him in charge of printing our publicity material. Hence, Communication Tsar!
Duncan Oh right.

Beat. Mel and Phoebe smile at Duncan

Phoebe That would be great. Thanks, Duncan.
Duncan Yes. I have to check.
Mel That would be really useful actually, Duncan.
Duncan Yes.
Jared But that's obviously not the only reason why you're here.
Jones We wanted you here.
Duncan Yeah, OK.

An awkward moment. Beat

Party   17

Jared OK, great, so the last name is the Peace in the Middle East Party.
Phoebe It'll get us headlines.
Mel But what if there's suddenly peace, what do we do then?
Phoebe It'll look like it was our idea.
Jared OK. So that's all the short-listed names, um, unless Duncan, you don't want to suggest a name do you?
Duncan Oh, no.
Jared OK. So let's all write down on the ——
Duncan Well how about The Friendly Party?
Jared Go on then. So the voting is between The Social Justice Party, The Righteous Party, Gladios, which is Latin for sword, The Peace In The Middle East Party and The Friendly Party.
Duncan This is very exciting. And is it just one vote each or ——
Jared Actually, yes good point ... let's do this *Weakest Link* style to avoid Duncan voting twice or something.

Jared addresses this to Mel, who takes pens and paper out of the top drawer in the cabinet and hands them out

So all write down *one* choice on the slips, we'll then count the votes.

They all pick up their pens and start to write. Heads down

Duncan So it's a new party?
Jared Yes.
Duncan Right. So I mean, no-one will actually ... vote for it, will they?

Beat. They look up. Duncan stares at his paper

Mel Yes of course they will!
Duncan Oh good-o. And is this for the next election then or ——
Jared Initially it was, Duncs, but we're now thinking that might be a bit of a squeeze time-wise, so we're aiming for the one after.
Mel At the latest.
Jones Hurry up then.
Jared Right, starting with Phoebe. Spooling to her right.
Phoebe The Peace in the Middle East Party.
Jones The Righteous Party.
Mel The Social Justice Party.
Jared We can't all have voted for our own names.
Mel Well what did you vote for?

Jared Gladios, Latin for sword.
Mel Tut. Jared.
Jared Well you voted for your one.
Phoebe Duncan?
Duncan I voted for the Righteous Brothers.
Jones Party! Yes!
Mel Oh for God's sake.
Jared Mel!
Mel It's a stupid name.
Jones Well it's our party's name now.
Phoebe We can't be called that.
Jones That's what the majority of us voted for.
Jared It's democratic. We have to do what's democratic.
Mel I don't think Duncan should be allowed to vote. He's only just turned up. He shouldn't have the same power as us.
Jones You're only saying that because he voted for my name.
Mel No I'm not. He shouldn't anyway.
Jared It's democratic, Mel. And looking at our beliefs page ...

Jared flips the chart. He goes past a page with "credit crunch??" on it, one with "celebs we know — Chris Barrie" on it, one with "olympics tie in?" on it, to a page marked "Beliefs." Underneath it are the words "Democracy" and "Space Program?"

 ... We have to go along with it.
Mel Right well, Duncan voted for The Righteous Brothers!
Jones You know what he meant though ——
Mel Which is not one of the nominated names, and is therefore a spoilt ballot. So your name only got one vote as well, and there is no winner. How's that for democratic?
Phoebe Oh well done, Mel.
Duncan Ah. Sorry, Jones.
Jared Yes, she's right about that, Jonesy.
Jones But you know what he meant!

Jones storms out of the shed, only reaching the doorway

Duncan If it makes things easier, I can change my vote to Gladios.
Jared (*reflex response*) Latin for sword?

Jones spins back in at the doorway

Jones No, don't do that, Duncan!

Party

Jones goes out of the shed and strides along outside the two windows on the back wall, clearly angry and cursing, but muted. He reaches the end and stops, head in hands

Jared Possibly the name is something we're not quite ready to tackle.
Duncan Sorry for bringing it up.
Jared Not your fault technically, Duncan.
Duncan Thanks.
Phoebe Let's take a quick break.
Duncan A half-time break.
Jared We're not having the cake yet, Duncan.
Duncan I didn't mean that. I just meant ... well why not?
Jared Because I said so.
Mel What do you mean you said so?
Jared Nothing.
Mel Don't try to make out like you're in charge or ——
Jared I'm not Mel. I was simply being firm but fair with Duncan.
Mel Because the leader has not been appointed yet ——
Jared Do you want Duncan to have the cake or not?

Jones approaches the window from outside. He glares at Mel and the coffee

Mel No, but ——
Jared Well what does it matter then?
Duncan Am I allowed some water?
Jared OK. Good. You can have some water.
Jones (*shouting from outside*) Look I really want some of that coffee.
Phoebe You can't.
Mel And you know that you can't.

Jones comes back in

Jones Jared, dude, can I —— ?
Mel Don't ask someone else, you've just been told no. That's classic male behaviour.
Jared Sorry, Jonesy, you can have water.
Jones But it's already ——
Mel But nothing — it's not Fairtrade.
Jones All right, but even so ——
Mel No, not even so. We're not drinking unfair trade coffee.
Phoebe I'll get rid of it.
Jones We've already made it, what difference does it make?

Mel It makes a difference to me.
Phoebe I'm getting rid of it.

Phoebe tries to leave. Jones grabs the coffee

Jones No, no wait.
Mel Put that coffee down this instant!
Jones Why didn't you realize it wasn't Fairtrade when you bought it?
Phoebe Because it's confusing, because there's a picture of poor workers on the packet so I assumed it was Fairtrade.
Mel Deceitful packaging.
Jones They're not exactly going to put a picture of a fat man in a bowler hat throwing money in the air on the packet are they?
Phoebe I've said I'm sorry.
Jared We're not drinking it.
Duncan Could we have tea instead?
Mel Or get some ethical coffee?
Jared Right, no to both of those questions. My mother is inside trying to do her Buddhist chanting. We're not going in to make tea or rummage for coffee. She'll go absolutely mental if we disturb her.
Mel Doesn't sound very Buddhist.
Jared That's why she does it. She has issues with her anger. Well actually, Dad has issues with her anger. She's absolutely fine with it.
Phoebe I'll get rid of the coffee.

Phoebe leaves

Jared follows her and stands by the door

Jared Not in the house!
Jones That's a terrible waste.
Mel Think of the African farmers.
Jones Don't tell me to think of the African farmers, I am constantly thinking of the African farmers.
Jared Simmer down please. You two. Again.

Phoebe comes back in, sans coffee pot

Duncan I'll pour the water.
Jared Thank you, Duncan.

Duncan walks over to the jug of water and fills everyone's glasses right to the top as the scene continues. The others say "thanks" "cheers Duncan" etc. as he fills their glass right to the top, holding them very carefully so as not to spill any. He fills Phoebe's glass last with only the tiny amount that was left in the jug. He stands a bit too close to her during this exchange. His crotch at eye level

Duncan Sorry.
Phoebe It's all right.
Duncan Um ... you can share mine.
Phoebe No I'd ... really rather not.
Jared OK. Good. Sit down, Duncan mate. (*After a beat*) Did you just pour that coffee on to the flowerbed, Phoebe?

Duncan sits. Mel stands to look at the flowerbeds

Phoebe It's fine.
Jared I'm not sure it is.
Mel You shouldn't give plants unfair trade coffee.
Jared I don't think the fairness of the trade is the issue here, Mel.
Jones I'm sure it's fine.
Jared Does anyone know anything about plants?
Duncan I worked in a garden centre once.
Jared Right. And?
Duncan We never gave them coffee.
Jones Don't think you pay for that coffee out of the party treasury by the way.
Phoebe No, fine, I won't.
Jones I'm not chipping in for that.
Duncan Ooh, what's the party treasury?
Jared (*pointing to the Thomas the Tank Engine money box on the table*) It's this Thomas the Tank Engine, Duncan.
Duncan Right. And is that valuable?
Jones It's a money box, Duncan.
Duncan I see. Just 'cos, isn't it really expensive to run for Parliament?
Jared Oh. Well, we're doing it for nothing, Duncan.
Duncan Right. Yes. We could get sponsorship!
Jared Keep talking.
Duncan Michael Swan got his World Challenge trip sponsored by ICI because Sally Webb's dad works there.
Jones That's interesting.
Mel Hang on a minute, we're setting up an anti-capitalist political party, we can't be sponsored by a sodding corporation.
Jones Are ICI unethical?
Duncan I don't see how they can be. They make paint.
Phoebe Do they test their paint on animals?

Duncan I think they test it on ... walls.
Mel I refuse to be sponsored by a corporation. It goes completely against everything we stand for.
Jared That's true actually. We're in favour of the more independent shops.
Duncan Like which ones?
Jared Well ... Monsoon? Is that ——
Jones It's a chain.
Jared Well look, I'm in favour of homemade paints! Made the traditional way.
Jones What's that?
Jared (*feel free to play here*) Grinding up ... you know ... berries to make red and stuff.
Jones Berries?
Phoebe I don't think that would work.
Jared Well not with that attitude, no.
Duncan Ooh. Have we got a colour? For the party.

No-one understands his point

Mel Colours don't matter, Duncan.
Duncan They do to the Green Party.

They see the sense in this

Jared It wouldn't hurt to think of a colour for the party actually.
Phoebe Good idea Duncan.
Duncan Oh really?
Jones They've mostly been used up.
Duncan Blue's gone.
Jones Red. Green. Yellow. Orange.
Phoebe Who's Orange?
Duncan The phone company.
Phoebe They're not a party.
Duncan No, but they kind of own that colour now.
Jared I think Plaid Cymru are Orange.
Mel Purple's the SNP.
Jones What colour are the BNP?
Duncan Black?
Jones That seems unlikely.
Phoebe We could be white!
Mel Yes. That's great. It's simple, like a fresh start.
Duncan And it would save a fortune on printing.

Party 23

Jared The danger is though, that people might think that, instead of us being the colour white, we might not have a colour — like be blank.
Jones Oh yeah, that's no good.
Phoebe I've got it. A rainbow. Like we're all the colours?
Mel Rainbow's fantastic!
Jared I like a rainbow.
Mel And it screams diversity.
Jones I have seen that somewhere before.
Jared Great.
Phoebe Let's go with a rainbow for now.

They vote. Four hands go up, everyone except Duncan

Duncan Purely in terms of printing costs, it doesn't get much worse than a rainbow.

They wait for Duncan's hand. It goes up

Jared Five. Great — we've finally got something to put on the proposals page.
Mel It's taken long enough.
Jared And I'm glad that it has, Mel. A rainbow is great.

Jared flips the chart on a page, empty but for the heading "Proposals"

Jones Someone else definitely uses it.
Phoebe It's what God uses to tell Noah the flood's over.
Jones Apart from that.

Jared writes "rainbow"

Jared Well if it's good enough for God, it's good enough for me. A rainbow will look lovely around our central message.
Duncan Oh — what's that?

Jared flips it on again to "central messages". It reads "Make everyone political" and "today"

Jared Well we've got two. There's "Make Everyone Political" which is to be worked on, um ... meanings-wise. Then there's Jonesy's phrase "Today".
Mel It's not a phrase.
Jones It is a phrase.

Mel It's one word.
Jones It's a one-word phrase.
Duncan Yes. What about "tomorrow"? Again, as a phrase?
Jared Ah, yes, like we're also working for the future.
Phoebe That's really nice actually.
Jared I think you may have stumbled on something rather good completely by accident there, Duncan.
Jones "Tomorrow, today." Combine them.
Phoebe Oh yes.

Jared starts to sing the McDonald's jingle. A silence falls. They look at Jared. Shocked

Jared You know my stance on McDonalds, guys, I have a T-shirt with 'McMurderers' on it.

Angry shouting from off stage. A woman's voice is screaming — telling someone to get out

Jones What the hell was that?
Jared That was my mother.
Duncan Is that one of her Buddhist chants?
Jared Um ... not that I know of, Duncan.

A voice is heard from off stage

Short Coat (*off*) Hello? Phoebe?
Jared Who's that?

Short Coat waddles in. He wears a very short coat and looks a bit sheepish

They freeze. He smiles at them

Phoebe Hi. Hi there.
Short Coat You all right?
Phoebe Yup.
Short Coat Hi everyone.

They all mumble something. Beat

Jones That's a nice short coat you're wearing.
Short Coat Oh. Thanks.

Party

Jones Aren't you going to introduce us, Phoebe?
Phoebe Um ... well, Mel, Martin, Jared and Duncan. This is ... (*She peters out as if she said a name*)
Short Coat Nathan.
Phoebe I said Nathan.
Jared Did you just disturb my mother, Nathan?
Short Coat I ... sorry, yes, I think so. I didn't know Phoebe would be ... in the shed.
Jared It's a summerhouse.
Short Coat Right. So ... what are you doing in here then?
Mel Nothing.
Short Coat Right.
Duncan We've formed a political party.
Short Coat Oh. Really?
Jared Yes.
Short Coat Cool. What's it called?
Duncan Not sure yet.
Short Coat Hmm. 'Cos I study Political Science if you want any advice or had any questions.
Jones We're all right for questions thanks, mate.
Jared Yes, it's answers we're after.
Short Coat Yeah. That's what I meant.
Duncan Um ... actually — do you know anything about Armenia?
Jared Duncan — don't —
Short Coat The capital's Yerevan.
Jared Whatever.
Short Coat It's high in sex trafficking.
Mel Is it?
Short Coat Oh yeah.
Mel Reinstate Armenia on to the spreadsheet please, Phoebe.
Jones Is sex trafficking where people meet in lay-bys and have sex?
Short Coat No, that's dogging.
Jones Yup, and what's the one where men meet in public toilets at night?
Short Coat That's cottaging.
Jones Yes, and what's the one where you, after you've come, you use a straw to sort of slurp up the —
Jared OK, Jonesy. That'll do.
Mel Disgusting.
Jared Sex trafficking doesn't involve cars necessarily, Jonesy — it's a bit of false friend. *Un Faux Amis*. We are going to discuss what our stance is on that at some point.
Short Coat Against it I'd imagine.

Jared Well we'll be the judge of that thank you ... mate.
Jones Also, um ... Short Coat ——
Short Coat It's Nathan!
Jones Yup, Nathan, um ... rainbow flags — who uses them?
Short Coat Gays.

Beat. Jared picks up his pen and goes to the flipchart

Jones Maybe cross out the ——
Jared Already doing it. (*He crosses out* 'rainbow' *and goes back to sit at the table*)
Short Coat So um ... Phoebe, do you want to do something later on or ... um ...
Phoebe Oh, um ... no.
Short Coat Right. Just 'cos, I've managed to get a couple of tickets to the Bodyworks exhibition, if ——

Jared stands and moves behind Phoebe

Jared It was a no, Nathan. We all heard her say it.

He puts his arm around her

Short Coat Phoebe, could we take this outside?
Mel We're not going to let you fight her.
Short Coat No, I didn't mean that.
Jared Would you like to go outside with Nathan, Phoebe?
Phoebe No.
Shot Coat Um, but ——
Jared You heard the lady, Nathan. Off you trot, mate.
Short Coat Mm. Good luck with the er ...
Jared Thank you.

  Shot Coat smiles and edges out

They watch him leave

Phoebe Oh, well done, Jared.
Mel What? That was totally sexist.
Jared Sometimes you have to be sexist, Mel. Sometimes sexist is the only language these bastards speak.
Phoebe I really ... hmmm — that was really very attractive what you just did.

Party

Mel What?
Jared Oh really?
Phoebe Yes, I ... hmmm.
Jared Oh. Well. What do you know.

Jared and Phoebe keep eye contact. She is demure

Mel Duncan, you really shouldn't tell people that we're setting up a political party. Then people might copy us and set up a rival party, and we don't want that.
Duncan Don't we want everyone to be political?
Mel Well yes, but we don't want everyone to be politicians. That wouldn't work.
Jones They can be political, as long as it's through the party.
Duncan Right. So what does being political mean?
Jones Voting for us.
Mel Well there's more to it than that!
Jones Not if I can help it there isn't. The public are cretins. The less they have to do with it the better.
Mel Excuse me — the public are not cretins.
Jones They are.
Jared A lot of them are pretty cretinous, Mel.
Mel Well we've got to make them less cretinous and more socially conscious.
Duncan Who's that?
Mel The ...
Jared Well ... the poor.
Mel Don't call them the poor!
Jared Hmm. All right — poor people.
Mel Yes, all right, that's slightly better.
Phoebe Well hang on. I'm poor you know.
Jared Mmm. You're not really.
Mel No you're not.
Phoebe I'm lower middle class at most.
Jared Well ...
Phoebe I am. My dad's a social worker and my mum's a hairdresser.
Jared Yeah, but ——
Jones It's her hairdressers.
Jared Exactly, and really it's more of a salon.
Mel You're hardly working class.
Jones There's no such thing as working class anymore.
Mel What?
Jones I read that.

Mel Well it's bullshit!
Jones Well I read it.
Phoebe I am.
Duncan So you don't like poor people?
Mel What?
Jones No, Duncan.
Phoebe Of course not.
Jared We love poor people. We're all about poor people.
Mel That's what this is about, Duncan. Helping people.
Jared Exactly. I'm a people person.
Mel We're all people people.
Duncan People people?
Mel Yes. Poor people people.
Duncan But you just said that they're greedy and stupid —
Jared Yes, but that's not their fault.
Duncan Oh right. So why is it them that need to change?
Jared Because, although it's not their fault that it happens, it is their fault that they do it. Because they're not aware of the shackles of consumerism.
Duncan Right. Um ...
Phoebe You can take a horse to water, Duncan.
Duncan Can you?
Phoebe Yes.
Mel The workers of this country are in the grip of the rich.
Duncan Are they?
Mel Yes.
Jared They are actually yes.
Duncan I mean, I work, but I'm not in the grip of the rich.
Jones No, not you, Duncan!
Jared Obviously not you, Duncan.
Phoebe You work?
Duncan Yes.
Phoebe What as?
Duncan I'm a Threshold Assessment Regional Deployment Officer.
Phoebe God how real.
Duncan Oh. Thanks.
Jared Is that why you're wearing the suit?
Duncan Yes.
Jones Are you allowed to wear that sexy skeletons tie to work?
Duncan Um ... well not normally no.
Mel I'm glad to hear it. It's a sexist tie.
Jones What do you mean "not normally"? Duncan?
Duncan Well, I am today.

Party

Jones Why?
Duncan Because it's ... my birthday.
Jones (*after a beat*) Is it?
Duncan Yes.
Jared
Mel } (*together*) Happy Birthday, Duncan/Duncs.
Phoebe

Jones starts to sing "Happy Birthday" but Jared gestures for Jones to stop singing

Jones (*speaking*) Duncan.
Duncan Thanks.
Phoebe So ... why did you come here?
Duncan Um ... because I was invited.
Jared Right.
Duncan And ... I thought maybe ... they might be connected. The party and ... my ...
Jared Oh. Hmmm. That's a bit um ...
Duncan It is a bit.
Mel I wish I'd known it was your birthday, Duncan, I'd have got you a pressie.
Duncan Oh. Well thanks, Mel. It's the thought that would have counted.

Awkward silence

Phoebe I mean, not exactly a present per se, but seeing as Duncan's got a job, we could make him Employment Secretary.
Jared Oh!
Jones Oh.
Mel No.
Phoebe He's sort of the most qualified.
Mel Mmm. Maybe we make him that until one of us gets a job, then we'll take over.
Duncan So I'll have two jobs.
Phoebe Yes, I've got two jobs.
Jones You haven't.
Phoebe I'm Secretary of State and also secretary of, you know, taking notes.
Jones Same thing, isn't it?
Phoebe No.
Duncan What are you, Jones?

Jones Well I'm Foreign Secretary, Duncan, because my mum's French.
Duncan Oh right. That makes sense.
Jones And also Sport.
Duncan Mel?
Mel I'm Cabinet Minister. And I'm also Health Secretary, because I have Irritable Bowel Syndrome.
Duncan Right. Is that a qualification or —
Mel It means I know a lot about health thank you, Duncan.
Duncan Um. Jared — what are ...
Jared In theory I'm Home Secretary, Duncan ... welcome ... but, you know ... I'm also —
Mel No, you're not.
Jared Well — I am really, Mel.
Phoebe No you're not.
Duncan What?
Jared You know ...
Duncan What?
Jared Leader.
Mel We haven't decided that.
Jared No I know.
Phoebe You're a minister like the rest of us.
Jared Yes, prime.
Mel No not prime.
Jared Well I mean, I'm the chairman of all the meetings and —
Mel Chairperson.
Jared I'm a man, Mel.
Mel But not all of us are.
Phoebe It's a sexist word.
Jared Only to women.
Jones We haven't voted on it yet.
Mel Exactly.
Jared No, I realize that, Jonesy, but the party does need a leader and I'm ready and willing.
Jones Well I'd like to put myself forward.
Mel Oh God no.
Jones Excuse me, why not?
Jared We've been through this, Jonesy — purely in terms of the party's young image, your hair is a bit ...
Jones I'm not going bald.
Jared Well ...
Jones My hair's just very feathery. It's a family thing.
Phoebe Have you tried giving it more body?

Jones Of course I've tried giving it more body!
Jared Come the next election, you will be bald, Jonesy, and as a leader that'd be no good at all —
Jones What? Why?
Jared People don't vote for bald leaders — look at what happened to Hague or (*pronouncing it phonetically*) Menzies Campbell.
Jones I am nothing like Menzies Campbell.
Mel It's Ming Campbell.
Jared What?
Mel It's pronounced Ming Campbell.
Jared Oh don't be ridiculous, Mel.
Mel It honestly is.
Jared Right. Yes. So, I'm going to go and buy some stationery from the shop John Ming.
Mel Well that's different.
Jared How convenient.

Phoebe stands and touches Jones's hair

Phoebe Even just sweeping it over might —
Jones (*standing bolt upright*) Touch my hair again and I'll neck you!
Phoebe God, calm down.
Jared Chill, Jonesy.
Mel Neck? That means kiss doesn't it?
Jones The other one then. Chin. I'll chin you.
Jared Well I don't think it's chin.
Jones I'll hit you. That's the point I'm making. You'll get hit.
Mel You'll hit a woman?
Jones No, I —
Phoebe That's an awful thing to say.
Jones I'll ... I'll go ape. (*He sits back down*)
Mel What does that mean?
Jones It means let's stop bloody talking about it.
Jared All right, Jonesy. Calm down.
Duncan Keep your hair on.

They laugh at this. Jones, stung, faces his chair away from them

Jared Very droll, Duncan.
Duncan Thanks. Sorry, Jones. But thanks to everyone else.
Jared So, look, my hair's not going anywhere, I'm a good figurehead, I'm comfortable in the limelight having done acting at school.
Duncan Ooh — what parts have you —

Jared Othello, Duncan.
Duncan Isn't Othello black?
Jared Traditionally yes, Duncan, but we couldn't do that at my school.
Mel You're not suitable, Jared.
Jared Oh come on.
Mel You're not.
Jared Well ... Why? Why not?
Mel Because —
Phoebe Don't, Mel.
Jared Don't what? Why ... not?

Beat. Mel is very solemn. She stands

Mel We find you quite sleazy.

Jones is interested in this. He begins to swing back round to face them

Jared What? No you don't.
Phoebe A little bit.
Jared I'm not sleazy. I'm tactile.
Mel It's a fine line.
Jared I've got the common touch.
Mel Well that's one way of putting it.
Jared You loved it a second ago.
Phoebe I got carried away. It won't happen again.
Mel Elaine said —
Jared Elaine spouts a lot of crazy shit!
Phoebe I just think it would be bad for our party to have a —
Jared What?
Phoebe Lothario as its leader.
Jared I'm not a Lothario!
Mel How many girls have you slept with this year?
Jared I'm not answering such questions.
Mel Prove us wrong then.
Jared All right. You'll have to give me a minute to tot it up.

Jared walks over to the door, to count on his fingers. Mel walks into the middle of the shed

Mel That speaks volumes. I, on the other hand have been political since the age of thirteen, I'm fully committed, I —
Jones (*standing*) No. No way. Don't even joke about it, Mel. You are not the leader.

Mel Excuse me — why not?
Jones Because you're really annoying.
Mel What? No I'm not!
Jones Well not to yourself, maybe but ——

Jared returns to the centre of the shed

Jared Eight!
Phoebe What?
Jared Only eight.
Mel That's loads.
Jared In the context of Nick Clegg it's peanuts.
Phoebe (*standing*) Well I think we can all agree that I'm a good compromise.
Mel Don't be ridiculous, Phoebe. You're far too nice.
Phoebe No I'm not.
Jones She really isn't.
Phoebe Thank you, Martin.
Jones It wasn't a compliment.
Duncan Shall we ... vote on it?

They look at each other for a second

Jared Yes. Come on then.
Jones Bring it.
Mel Fine.
Phoebe Lovely.
Jared We need to get this sorted out.
Phoebe So do we just vote or ——
Jared We should do a hostings.
Mel Hustings.
Jared Hostings.
Mel It's pronounced ——
Jones Let's just do it please. (*He heads over to a small box by the armchair*)
Jared All right, Jonesy.
Phoebe How does hustings work?
Jared We each say why we should be leader.
Jones (*placing the box directly underneath the lightbulb*) On there.
Jared Quickly though.
Mel Fine.
Phoebe Well how quickly?
Mel Just a few words.

Duncan So how many?
Mel Hundred.
Jones Not a hundred.
Jared Less than a hundred.

Beat

Duncan Three?
Jones Three's good.
Mel Three's not enough.
Jared Scared you can't do it in three?
Mel I can do it in three.
Jones So let's do three then.
Mel Fine.
Jones Right. Three words. Why we should vote for you. (*Pointing at the stool*) On there.
Phoebe Who starts?

They look at the box. Jones and Mel are closest. They begin to move towards it, when Jared suddenly springs his leg forward, stepping on the box from some distance. He slides along the floor with his trailing leg

Jared I'll start. (*He stands up straight, his hair almost touching the lightbulb. He feels the heat from it and looks up, before regaining composure*)
Mel Well go on then, Jared.
Jared All right I'm thinking.
Mel I can go first if —
Jared No I've got it. Write these down please, Phoebe.
Phoebe Yes I will.
Jared OK so ...
Mel Come on, Jared.
Jared (*shouting*) Kind!
Phoebe That's one.
Jared Strong, and —
Mel That's three.
Jared "And" doesn't count.
Mel It's three words.
Jones Not "and" though.
Jared And clever.
Mel No — don't write down clever, Phoebe, you've had your three words, Jared.
Jared Oh come on, Mel.

Mel No, that's your three words.
Jared Well that's ——
Mel That's the rules. Phoebe?

Jared climbs off the box, dismayed. He sulks over to the door. Phoebe stands from behind the table and walks over to the box and steps on to it

Phoebe (*declaring with some confidence*) Progress. Healthcare. Schemes.
Jones What do you mean schemes?
Phoebe As in schemes. I have schemes.
Jones What schemes have you got?
Jared All right, Jonesy, that'll do. Mel?

Phoebe get off the box and returns to her seat, as Mel walks over to the box, steps on it and steadies herself

Mel Passionately.
Jones (*to Jared*) Well passionately's a waste.
Jared (*disapproving*) Jonesy.

Mel is offended by the interruption and quickly goes to start again

Mel Passionately.
Jones So that's passionately twice!
Mel No, I was repeating my first word.
Jared (*seizing on this*) Ah no, Mel, sorry those are the rules. You said passionately twice.
Mel Why would I want passionately twice?
Jared Those are the rules. You made me have "and". You made me have "and"!

Jared and Jones are ecstatic

Jones Final word!

Just as she is about to say it, Phoebe interrupts her

Phoebe Good luck.
Mel Liberal. (*She steps off the box*)
Phoebe Martin?

Jones gets on. Very confident

Jones Yes. We.
Mel (*ridiculing him*) Oh, not "yes we can"!
Jones (*defensively*) I wasn't going to say yes we can.
Mel Don't try to compare yourself with Obama!
Jones I wasn't going to do that.
Mel OK — so what were you going to say?
Jones Something else.
Mel So go on then. Yes. We.
Jones (*after a beat*) May.
Phoebe Yes we may?
Jones Yup. (*He gets off the box*)
Jared Right, so now we ——
Phoebe Well hang on Duncan hasn't done his yet.
Jared Oh yes, go on, Duncan.
Duncan Oh, but I don't want to ——
Mel You have to do it anyway, Duncan.
Jones Just say anything, Duncan.
Duncan Um. No. Thanks.
Jared One more word, Duncs.

Jared picks up the box for Duncan to touch it and say his final word

Duncan Please.
Jared Good lad.
Mel Right. Read them back, Phoebe.
Phoebe OK — so we've got "kind strong and", "progress healthcare schemes" "passionately passionately liberal", "yes we may" and "no thanks please."
Jared I'm not sure the hostings has been that useful.
Mel Hustings.
Jones How are we voting?
Phoebe Each vote for your favourite choice as leader and ——
Jones We'll just get a stalemate again ——
Mel We'll go with the Single Transferable Vote system and you can't vote for yourself. So you number your choices one to four in order of preference. It's impossible to get a draw.
Jared Fine.

Jones gets a pile of papers and pens from the filing cabinet and passes them around

Jones OK. Let's vote.

They all write

Duncan It's not very nice ranking people, is it?
Jared No one will take it personally, Duncan.
Mel Stop talking please.
Jared Why?
Mel It could be code for telling him how to vote.
Jared Of course it's not code.
Mel Anything could be code.
Jones So that could be code?
Mel Of course that's not code!
Jones Or this could be code?
Mel Shut up!
Phoebe Right, pass them to me if you've finished and I'll do the official count.

They all pass her their votes. Duncan gives his in last. Jared starts pacing around the stage in expectation. As do Jones and Mel. Duncan watches them and finally gets up and also starts pacing

Duncan I have no idea what's going on.
Mel Right, Duncan, over fifty per cent is a victory. No votes and you're eliminated. Under fifty per cent and we go to second choice.
Jones Over fifty per cent means three votes right?
Mel When it's this small a poll, yes.
Phoebe (*reading the papers*) You can't vote for yourself, Duncan.
Duncan What? No I know.
Phoebe Who put Duncan first?
Mel It's a secret ballot.
Jared Did you put Duncan first?
Mel I'm not answering that — it's a secret ballot.
Jared Why did you do that?
Jones Because she didn't want to vote for us because we might win. It's dirty.
Jared That's low, Mel.
Mel It's tactical.

Phoebe stands, looking at the results. They gather round

Phoebe So looking at our first choices, the results of the official count are: Duncan got one, Jared got two ——

Jared Come on.
Phoebe Jones got one and Mel got one. So I'm eliminated. Brilliant. Thanks guys.
Mel No majority, so we keep going.
Jared Second choices then, Phoebe.
Phoebe Right. Oh I got three!
Mel But you're already out.
Phoebe (*stung*) OK. So. One for Mel. (*After a beat*) And one for Duncan.
Jones Duncan? So I'm ——
Phoebe You're eliminated.
Jones (*to Duncan*) Oh you prick!
Duncan Sorry. Jonesy.
Jones Sorry, sorry. Duncan.
Mel So it's two, two, two.
Jared Third choices then, come on, Phoebe.
Phoebe (*looking at the papers*) Right, so, no votes for Mel.
Mel What? Really? Recount!
Jones What do you mean recount?
Mel I'd like a recount please.
Phoebe OK. No votes for Mel.
Mel So what — I'm eliminated?
Jones Welcome to my world.
Phoebe Two for Jones.
Jones (*sarcastically*) Right. Brilliant.
Jared So ...?
Phoebe One vote for Jared.
Jared Yes — that's three!

Jared high fives Jones. Jones starts goading Mel. Jared is very pleased

Jones Yes!
Jared At bloody last.
Jones Always wanted you to win.
Jared Oh thanks, mate ——
Phoebe And two votes for Duncan.

Beat

Jared What?
Mel Not really?
Duncan Oh. What?
Jones Let me see that.

Jared How can Duncan get ——
Jones Did you vote for Duncan?
Jared Well rather than vote for these two, yeah. Did you?
Jones Well yeah, but ——
Phoebe So Duncan got four.
Duncan Did I?
Jared But, I mean, hang on ——
Mel So what does that mean?
Phoebe Mathematically — um ... four is higher than three.
Duncan I don't think I should be leader.
Mel Yes, I think that's bloody obvious, Duncan.
Jared Well what do we do now?
Phoebe It's democratic.
Mel But it's a mistake.
Phoebe It can't be. It's democratic.
Jones Hang on. This can't happen.
Phoebe Yes. I mean it has.
Jones I mean, we can't let this happen.
Jared You're saying we interfere with the vote?
Jones Well no, but ——
Mel Well then.
Jones But just this once.
Mel I don't think the phrase "just this once" can really be applied to rigging elections.
Duncan Right. I mean, I don't really want to be leader.
Jared Yes, that's irrelevant, Duncan.
Duncan Oh. 'Cos, you all quite want to be. So ... do it again if ...

Mel flips the chart back to the "beliefs" page

Phoebe No. Democracy is effectively the only thing we've got on the beliefs page. If we start tampering with that then ... well we're only left with the Space Program and that's not exactly a belief anyway.
Jared And I'll be honest, I don't think we'd be able to afford it. Hence the question mark.
Duncan So I mean ... nobody's happy with that are they?
Jones It's not ideal certainly.
Jared No, but that's what it is.
Jones What what is?

Beat

Jared The situation.

Duncan I don't understand.
Jared No. It's sort of ... the system.
Mel That's the best system we've got.
Duncan Right. Could I resign?
Mel Yes!
Phoebe Oh good idea, Duncan, you could resign.
Jared And then we do it again.
Jones But this time don't vote Duncan to stop other people getting votes!

They return to the table to find paper and pens

Jared Yes. Good. Right, so, everyone get a pen and ——
Duncan Hang on a sec.
Jared What is it?
Duncan I haven't resigned.

Beat. They stop and look at him

Mel But you said you would ——
Duncan No. I just asked if I could. I don't think I will.
Jones Um ... you're not going to?
Duncan No thank you, Jones. I don't think I will.
Jared So what do you want to do, Duncan?

Duncan gestures to the chairs. They sit and look at him

Duncan Well let's start with that cake.

BLACK-OUT

FURNITURE AND PROPERTY LIST

On stage: Rickety table. *On it*: papers, pens, BlackBerry, Thomas the Tank Engine money box, large glass jug of water, screw-top bottle of red wine, empty glasses for **Jones**, **Phoebe** and **Duncan**
Filing cabinet. *On it*: pot of coffee, empty glasses for **Jared** and **Mel**. *In top drawer*: pens, piles of paper
Plush, comfortable armchair. *By it*: small box
Wheelie office chair
3 fold-out or plastic garden chairs
Flipchart which reads "credit crunch??" on open sheet. *On flipped over sheets*: first page: "celebs we know — Chris Barrie"; second page: "olympics tie in?"; third page: "Beliefs" with " Democracy" and "Space Program?" underneath; fourth page: "Proposals"; fifth page: "Make everyone political" and "today".
On stand: board pen

LIGHTING PLOT

Practical fittings required: light bulb hanging from ceiling

Interior. The same scene throughout

To open: Practical on with covering spots, daylight through windows and doorway

No cues

EFFECTS PLOT

No cues

Lightning Source UK Ltd.
Milton Keynes UK
UKOW06f2059221117
313187UK00013B/746/P